POEMS
With A
MESSAGE

RAY LOHMAN

authorHOUSE·

AuthorHouse™
1663 Liberty Drive
Bloomington, IN 47403
www.authorhouse.com
Phone: 833-262-8899

Published by AuthorHouse 09/28/2020

ISBN: 978-1-7283-7277-8 (sc)
ISBN: 978-1-6655-0155-2 (e)

Print information available on the last page.

New King James Version (NKJV)
Scripture taken from the New King James Version®. Copyright © 1982 by Thomas Nelson. Used by permission. All rights reserved

New International Version (NIV) Holy Bible, New International Version®, NIV® Copyright ©1973, 1978, 1984, 2011 by Biblica, Inc.® Used by permission

The Holy Bible, Berean Study Bible, BSB Copyright ©2016, 2018 by Bible Hub Used by Permission. All Rights Reserved Worldwide.

CONTENTS

REFLECTIONS

SPORTS

HISTORY

WISDOM

POLITICS

ENDINGS

FOREWORD

Poetry was the least of my plans to stay mentally active in my senior years. Having given up sports or and most physical activities, and after surviving the Harvey disaster, and spending months rebuilding the interior of our home, I suddenly found myself without any productive activities to look forward to. When watching TV one day I recognized that so many programs I was watch were often interrupted by all kinds of bad news, thus constantly destroying my peaceful solitude. I found myself being interrupted by negative thoughts too often. So, I decided to write my feelings about this in a poem. Hence, my first poem, "My Solitude" was born. That was so much fun and the message it relayed, I'm sure many could relate too. I decided to try to write another poem with a message and found it was something I could do; it passed the time, lots of which I had available and it was at times, mentally challenging.

I read a few poems in a poetry book and found too many of them lacking understandable meanings or messages, at least for me. The message to me was clear, if I write poems, they will make sense and will usually carry a message of courtesy, morality, a vision of nature or God. This booklet of poems may be the end of my writing for reasons only God can explain. I am now 89 years old and have been writing only 2 years. I know He had a lot to do with my decision to write, and expected me to use His name occasionally. In fact, I did use it quite often, as it became my opportunity to do something productive. And I thank God for the brain He let me retain at these later years of my life.

Sorry if my poems are too amateurish, but remember, they were all produced by a true amateur, but with God's help. Hope you find some you can enjoy.

Thanks to my Grandson, Andrew Crocker for helping me get started writing with a small measure of poetry structure.

Ray Lohman

NATURE

FOREST, A SONNET

A trip through the forest so soothes the soul,
with sounds of silence defining the mood.
Mindful of nature providing the goal,
of lending a concept of gratitude.

Sunlight filters through many shapes of leaves.
Shadows dance merrily with every move.
Seeing figures, images to believe,
scary thoughts of a mysterious ghoul.

Whispering breezes send echoes of love,
to objects unknown, lacking a presence.
Hearing a concert of birds from above,
feeling intrusive by my existence.

Forests exist in God's wonderful world,
providing beauty of visions unfurled.

WINDS

Silently, the winds seek a resting place,
whistling through fallen, rusty autumn leaves.
Producing a sound while filling a space
where whispers so often try to deceive.

Creating messages without an end.
Swirling strong breezes transmit a weird sound,
seeking, to find hearers sharing the wind.
Hearing small whispers while searching the ground,

Silence can carry a rueful message,
whispering often leaves moments of strife.
Presence of strong winds searching for passage,
leads many to find new values in life.

Seeking new knowledge our main concern,
searching the winds for new lessons to learn.

MY OLD OAK TREE

History is stored in my old oak tree,
swinging from branches many years ago.
Little did I know how strong it would be?
nor how big it would be after full growth.

We played around big limbs after they grew,
into odd shapes, not useful for lumber.
Roots rising from ground as if they knew,
kids had fun in its shade in hot summer.

Showing their strength as they rose to the sky,
beauty of twisted limbs shaped over time.
Changing the landscape, so nice to the eye,
God's creation, nature clearly defined.

Leaving the old tree after I grew older,
another memory it seemed to know,
times will change to make us both bolder.
Our shapes do evolve with new looks to show.

Sometimes I think, if I could be buried,
under my friend, this beautiful old tree,

we could live together, never hurried.
God did not plan this, it will never be.

Returning to visit my huge oak tree,
It's clear, my passing, it will live to see.

CLOUDS

Those mysterious objects, in the sky,
shifting winds, making unusual sights.
Ever changing images, catching an eye,
strangely pleasing, often shading the light.

As we ponder, the source of such beauty,
moving images creating new thought.
Separating us, from our routine duty,
envisioning life that cannot be bought.

Imagining thoughts, of dreams unfulfilled,
minds ever reaching, a faraway place.
Clouds, clearly the source, of undefined skill,
mysterious dreams, our hearts can embrace.

God gave us clouds, for mankind to know,
such pleasure in life, only He can bestow.

SILENCE, A SONNET

The gift of silence, always a blessing,
all pleasures of sound, now quietly mute.
Walking in forests, with no wind stirring,
at early daylight, when shadows can't move.

A voice in my mind, talking in soft tones,
silence fills the air, birds not yet singing.
God fills my soul, I know I'm not alone,
speaking with pleasure, His voice is ringing.

Thanks to our God for the gift of silence,
sweet sounds of His voice fill a grateful soul.
Comforting thoughts He provides make true sense,
certain His blessings will never grow old.

Freedom to hear our loving God speak,
messages I know will be ours to keep.

THE SLEEPY RIVER

A quietly sleepy stream, calm as it flows,
always on call there, and willing to serve.
Completing some special purpose, who knows,
many unique values, fully deserved.

Streaming by valleys, and down deep caverns,
creating great sprays, and shooting down falls.
Swallowed by calm lakes, or greedy oceans,
ending all value, it finished its call.

REPRISE

Rains arriving, dark storms begin to build,
muddy waters rising, to unsafe levels.
Weak structures fail, to survive nature's will,
destruction came, as if by the devil

Plans to contain, as usual not there,
waters reaching, creating such terror.
Many lives lost, by flooding everywhere,
failure to manage, exposed big errors

Rivers, so useful, as often revealed,
having a conscience, too often concealed.

WEATHER

The wind, the rain, white snow, ice and sun,
weather conditions can make one think twice.
It can be trouble but also much fun,
And playing inside can be very nice.

High flying kites, in an extra strong wind,
often produces, excitement at play.
Joy interrupted, when cold rains begin,
onset of snow, brings a cold winter day.

Snow can provide, good things for pleasure,
bad weather can also, produce good times.
Sledding, skiing, snowballs for good measure,
sun brightens our spirits, opens our minds.

It's right back to play, when bad weather ends,
great times of fellowship, with all my friends.

TREES

We have on earth, so much to see
But nothing in all of nature's scenes
Can please as much as colorful trees
Many great views there to be seen

Mountains streams valleys forests
All so pleasing to the viewer's eye
Providing nice pictures for the purist
Views of trees that rise to the sky

Late seasons bring so many colors
Maples yellow leaves shining so bright
Small tallow trees blend like no other
Beauty that fades In darkness of night

Forests so green completes the view
Background, colors, oh such splendor
Leaves in the morn shining with dew
Such beauty does nature alone render

Fall and cold winter begins in the hills
Dark forests still with only one sound
Falling leaves gently beginning to fill
Undefined spots on dark, cold ground

Sunrise brings a bright morning sky
Dawn filters light with a small breeze
Such visions of beauty pleases the eye
Scenes our Lord designed from trees

PEOPLE

A GOOD FATHER

A special name which to all means so much
Great companion to the woman he loves
Leading his siblings with a loving touch
Conflicts are handled with gentle kid gloves

Serving family with loving compassion
Enjoying successes as if his own
Failures are met by teaching a lesson
His voice so strong yet always a soft tone

Setting examples with a life so pure
Showing good effort in all endeavors
Explaining to all how one can be sure
A family leader now and forever

Fathers will always be placed number one
In minds of their siblings under the sun

PEOPLE WE HAVE KNOWN

How our lives change by people we have known.
Most gave us knowledge, we proudly have shown.
Sadly, some people teach ways not the best,
some will be led to be worse than the rest.

Hearing of God's love is always so good,
Learning his Word, not always understood.
Finding His truths of which there are many,
life is worth living since there are plenty.

What a wonderful world, His creation,
sharing our joy and sometimes elation.
Every day we can seek new endeavors,
knowing we have His true love forever.

Releasing our passion for God alone,
Expecting to know Him when we go home.

A SONNET FOR MOTHERS

God's special gift to all is our mothers,
Always being so helpful to others,
quietly sharing themselves with their love ones.
solving the problems encountered by sons

Daughters are God's way to please sweet mothers,
Lifetime companions, loving each other,
their closeness so tender their bonds so tight.
meeting sadness or joy with clear insight

Nothing in life, so sweet as a mother,
Seeking ever to guide a dear brother,
consoling, searching for ways to support.

always striving to give glowing reports.
Mothers, so precious, only God can claim.
God's angels not seeking fortune or fame.

LUKE

Youngest of the rising golf stars I've known,
his statuesque build is made for the sport.
So pure of stature and strength he owns,
his perfect golf swing, easy to report.

With drives so certain, and always so long,
his demeanor, sure, yet full of meaning.
Projecting a message, that's seldom wrong,
winning matches, always a good feeling.

Response to challenges, he clearly loves,
always so poised, not showing his thoughts.
A promise of honors, descends from above,
skill of God's making, for matches well fought.

A vestige of talent, others can't claim,
many can only, relate in their dreams.
Admirers gather, to show their acclaim.
Expectations of wonderful things, it seems.

Ready for upsets that might come his way,
Remember, God always controls the play.

LOVING LIFE'S WAY

What is it about her I revere today?
So happy, yet clearly, so strong of mind.
Is it her exotic, mysterious way,
Often so loving, to me always kind.

Too many busy days away, for my taste,
to share ongoing simple expressions.
Our times are special, too precious to waste,
of love and trust, in daily sweet sessions.

Who knows, what secret tomorrow holds?
Pleasant memories past, wondrous events.
Life's ongoing measures, can make us old,
slowly fading, as our old age presents.

How love of life, gets more trivial as,
we spend more time, on simple survival.

MY BROTHER TED AND I

My brother and I lived, a tough start in life,
together we shared, unpleasant events.
Absence of parents, to guide our ways right,
until grandparents came, for sure God sent.

Grandmother was like, an angel on earth;
Our uncles and aunts, just teenagers still,
Grandad's stern ways, helped reveal our true worth.
kept us involved, all a part of God's will.

Sharing a home, so strong in character,
and the family's, enduring deep love,
helped us mature, in all things that matter.
Life clearly for us, God's gift from above.

Their love for us, was deeply apparent,
our lives worth living without our parents.

MY BROTHER TED

To not many men, was god so gracious,
As he was to my dear brother ted.
His gifts, so abundantly precious,
Though a life, not always easily led.

As young boy, in music he excelled,
His clarinet, produced heavenly sounds.
At age fifteen, on hard times he fell,
But his talents grew, by leaps and bounds.

Then another talent, came clear to all,
Offering support for family's needs.
He managed a store, no problem at all,
His work in metals, and oils grew indeed.

Beginning a career, and passtime as well,
His creative mind, was sure to succeed.
Talents, and speaking, soon known by others,
The beautiful life, led by my brother.

REPRISE TO TED

My poem about Ted, left much to be said;
his talents and character so greatly defined.
There's much more about him that must be read,
his gifts from God were so clearly designed.

To bring joy and much pleasure to others,
the attributes he so strongly revealed.
That's why I'm so proud to be his brother,
his clarinet provoked excitement so real.

His works of art shown in so many places,
showing such skills in style and creation.
The talent he so clearly embraces,
leaving these skills he took up another.

Restoring relics of ancient weapons,
creating new parts, making one wonder,
what gift was he next destined to make,
when his beautiful soul God chose to take.

WHAT MORE COULD I ASK

Things I enjoyed, this season of seasons,
worship through great music, and word.
What more could I ask, at this time?

Sunday dinner, shared with loved ones.
Great sporting events there to enjoy.
What more could I ask, at this time?

My thoughts cannot, adequately explain,
a peaceful home, loved ones to cherish.
What more could I ask, at this time?

Moments of reflection, enter my mind,
to be born in America, God is so kind.
What more could I ask, at this time?

Events, news, many ideas to consider,
freedom to choose, limited distractions.
What more could I ask, at this time?

Pleasures with, so many special friends.
Character, numbers, all mine to select.
What more could I ask, at this time?

My Lord has so abundantly, blessed me,
years, good health, beyond expectations.
What more could I ask, at this time?

My only regret, is leaving my loved ones.
God's promises, make our future divine.
What more could I ask, at this time?

BELLA

A happy young lady, her life so filled,
support from God's love, it's easy to tell.
A beautiful person so very skilled,
so strong of heart, mind and body as well.

Belief in herself to excel as she dreams,
gymnastics skills, so amazing they please.
Cheering in tandem with a great team,
Double flips with double twists done with ease,

Serious about her love for her Jesus,
talents received, to influence friends.
Most activities designed to please us,
hoping always, her joy would never end.

Times spent for fun, partying with girlfriends,
maturing as a sweet teenager should.
Now sharing these times, with
handsome boyfriends,
life led by God, is wonderfully good.

A future so bright in many great ways,
Lights shine from Heaven defining her days.

GOOD TIMES

They were four years old, she was his best friend.
As they grew older, their minds did mature,
he assumed he would know her, until the end.
Their respect and friendship seemed to endure.

Maturing led to, more serious attempts,
to strengthen their effort, to recall events.
but, mature minds, and, diversions of thought,
made it hard to restore, what they had sought.

Sad feelings they felt, as they had to part.
A simple romance, too many years past.
Too many things, they just couldn't restart,
even their friendship, not like the last.

They knew separation, had taken a toll,
good memories survived, as they grew old.

A VALENTINE SONNET

Flowers, Candy, and love, from the Heart,
promises kept, at least fun for a day.
Believing our message, never to part,
thinking forever, be always this way.

Tradition derived from Saint Valentine,
enhancing a lifetime, for lovers to play.
Revealing affection, always be mine,
friendships, forever, not ending today.

Another long year to renew my joy,
dreaming of that day I'll see him again.
No longer a child, today a grown boy,
someday I hope his intentions are plain.

God, hear my prayers, let my dreams come true,
Our Lord will determine what he will do.

HUMILITY

What decisions can I make today?
To make friends who sometimes say
He is a humble man in every way

Credits are given, none expected
Never angry, but calm, respected
Softly spoken even when rejected

Needing wise choices above all else
Always certain when making a point
Seeking progress, but not for my self

Listen to facts when clearly defined
Seeking real answers, not foolish calls
Hearing all patiently and always kind

Standing for each one's right to speak
Always avoiding words to find fault
Hear all ideas, both strong and weak

Words with clear meaning revealed
Approval is sought from all involved
Always positive when making a deal

Removing one's self as part of the call
Valuable answers are usually gained
Peers can share and agree with it all

My lead to start often may not be best
Avoid above all, any unneeded stress
Humility's magic can lead to success.

ANNABELL

Youngest of the upcoming stars I know,
voices rise, as her beauty is about
such perfect stature, her face shining glow,
All eyes gather, for her grand coming out.

Her smile, so certain about its meaning,
motions, responses, ring clearly of love.
Protected, poised, not showing her feelings,
promise of favors, descends from above.

An angel of God's making, so it seems,
a vision of beauty, none else can claim.
Others can only relate in their dreams,
admirers gather, to hail their acclaim.

Sweet ringlets of gold, frame her striking face,
made perfect by her God's redeeming grace.

A CHILD IS ILL

A child is ill it is so sad to see,
our hearts goes out, so filled with sympathy.
Yet fever lingers on and on

The little one does not understand why
parents try hard to comfort, as they cry.
Yet fever lingers on and on

The night is filled with nurses being sure,
their care provides the best known ways to cure.
Yet fever lingers on and on

We question why this sweet innocent one
suffers for no reason under the sun.
Yet fever lingers on and on

Many prayers are being lifted today.
The sickness, we hope, will no longer stay.
Yet fever lingers on and on

With faith, believe, His timing must prevail,
Great is God's mercy, healing will not fail.

MEMORIES

Silently finding, clear thoughts of the past,
pleasures of time, are now closing the door.
August days, leaving memories that last,
lingering regrets, for not sharing more.

Searching my mind, before it's too late,
recalling so many, windows of sadness.
My fading mind, was in such a sad state,
I forgot my God, brought so much gladness.

When did I discover, life's real meaning,
measures so empty, 'til reaching the end.
Now clear, it was only the beginning,
of time for a meeting, with my old friends.

Heaven remains a mystery to me
I'm only certain my soul will be free.

QUEENIE

A story often told, always with joy,
a fuzzy bundle of fun and pleasure.
It starts with a little dog and a boy,
over the years a wonderful treasure.

Growing up, their friendship grew very strong,
enjoying good times, surviving the bad.
Sharing much, not ever apart for long,
comforting each other when one was sad.

Because of war, Queenie's friend left home,
she could never understand, what went wrong.
Suddenly, her best friend left her alone;
hours passed to days, all became so long.

Years passed by, her master did not return,
yet, living for something, she knew not why.
There came days when she no longer yearned,
but never forgetting, even when she tried.

New friends became an unhappy pastime,
her heart was not into sharing their fun.
Living seemed only, for sad days to pine,
nothing could replace, her happy long runs.

One quiet day, sleeping on her earth pillow,
she was awakened by a distant sound.
Was she dreaming, did she hear a whistle,
sounding so clearly, her master was found!

Running eagerly, her heart was pounding.
Up the dirt road, at the distant curves end,
believing now, her master made the sound.
With arms open wide, he greeted his friend.

A bark and a leap, she was in his arms,
her long lost master had, at last, returned.

BEST FRIENDS

They asked for nothing, nothing was denied,
separation never altered their friendship.
To rely on each other, it's assurance untried,
happiness shared brought forth a great kinship.

Their lives seem to be made in the same mold,
one never questioned the other's core feelings.
Clear thoughts and demeanor as they grew old,
Left no doubt about personal dealings.

Demands on their lives, often revealing,
certain measures they join in reflection.
Willing to share most intimate feelings,
standing against life's unfair rejections.

Finding their way with God's pure instructions,
lasting friendships, without interruption.

MY SOLITUDE

Upon my couch I oft decline,

To view a part of life sublime,

And see an actor's sense of history,

Playing a part in TV mystery.

Oh see the commercial's perfect schemes,

To solve my problems, sell my dreams.

But then, my pleasure, sore-ly interrupted,

By politics, so vile, corrupted,

Of wars, murders, rapes and kidnapping,

My peace destroyed, these interlocutory trappings.

Distasteful, wasteful, meaningless interludes,

Destroyers of my sublime solitude.

Life can be too often rude

My First Poem

THANKSGIVING

What makes Thanksgiving such a pleasure,
remembering times when we were younger.
Relatives, good food, friendships to treasure,
feasting 'til never more will we hunger.

Hearing each other's recent history,
so many stories each wants to relate.
As expected there are no mysteries,
revealing our thoughts 'til it's very late.

Knowing often, we only share wishes,
to see a faraway loved one or brother.
We hungrily savor so many dishes,
While dining, plans, to visit each other.

Sharing with loved ones we wish would not end,
Thanksgiving, God's gift for family and friends.

HOMECOMINGS

Homecomings can be such fun to attend,
faces remembered, others test our minds.
Stories embellished, seemed never to end,
seeing old friends, aging has not been kind.

Losing old friends, from whatever reason,
reminds us of our own life and our future.
We realize we're also, in our late season,
but enjoying fun, with friends we nurture.

Activities so planned, we fear a mistake,
leads us to wonder, what we're doing now.
Enjoying the party, for goodness sake,
our abilities tested, we don't know how.

We don't remember, since passing of time,
showing our skills, there's not much left of mine.

MY ONE LOVE

Sweetest of the special rising star I know,
a young voice of beautiful favors to shout.
So pure of stature and with a shining glow,
all eyes gathered to share her coming out.

Her smile is always certain about its meaning,
smooth motions, responses, ring clearly of love.
Projecting, poised, never showing her feelings,
sweet promise of favor, decending from above.

An angel of God's making, so clearly it seems
His creation of beauty, none other can claim.
Observers can only relate in their dreams,
admirers strain, longing to gain her acclaim.

Sweet ringlets of golden hair frames her face
She is made perfect by God's redeeming grace.

REFLECTIONS

SEARCHING

Often we search, for God's wisdom in life,
we heard of His coming, one glorious day.
We seek God's blessing, as always we strive,
to live like His Son, who showed us the way.

Always remember, He came as a babe,
willing to heed, leads us never to waver.
God's plan for His life, so many to save,
the joy of knowing, we have his favor.

Believing helps us, to do some things good;
His presence leads, to a joyful, good life.
Knowing He is there, we find brotherhood,
though problems arise, there remains no strife.

"Let every tongue acknowledge our Lord"
seeking our Savior, has never been hard.

WHISPERING

A small voice talking, without being asked,
sometimes It's strange, as It speaks so meekly.
Quietly revealing, when things are unmasked,
it seems so clear, it knows me completely.

Daily, It tells me, when things are all right,
whispers from God, are always so useful.
Without searching, we're always in His sight,
He clears up thoughts, by being so truthful.

Correcting our faults, is one of His aims,
sharing good ideas, without being told.
Providing a message, I cannot claim,
but seeking to show me, a worthy goal.

God's Holy Spirit, constantly guides me,
He lives within me, I'll always be free.

WONDERS

Wonderful treasures, our God has created,
sometimes they seem beyond our belief.
Events from God, leaves us always elated,
pure healing wonders, gives needed relief.

What mysteries make the sky seem blue,
and forests so many bright shades of green?
God's miracles we believe to be true,
He created natures beautiful scenes.

Bluebonnets rising across a hillside,
sun flowers fill a glorious picture.
Creations of God for all to decide,
Wonders like these, we simply call nature.

Small Islands r(sing, from brilliant blue seas,
volcanoes emerge from oceans so bold
White sands surrounding the tallest palm trees,
mountains revealing God's powers of old

Winters exposing bright layers of snow,
covering nature, with blankets of white.
Sunshine providing a beautiful glow,
shadows of nightfall erasing the light

Marvelous images, in our world reveals,
some we believe, might exist forever.
It is true, God's eternal plan is sealed,
the source of man's magnificent treasures.

Multitudes of wonders, today exist,
our God's creations, too many to list.

SONGS OF LOVE

Songs of love, embraced in unending time,
resplendent sounds, colorful joyous refrains.
Delighting the soul as she lifts her voice,
melodious tones, of magical charm.

Swallows circling in a warm autumn sky,
winds reshaping the billowing white clouds.
Trumpets and strings passionately clashing,
instruments flaring defining new sounds.

Her voice is lifted, quieting the clamor,
music from the heart, misty words of love,
a love song defined, so fondly fulfilled,
of twilight whispers, lovingly lifted.

Songs of passion, so strongly revealing,
floating sweet designs with smooth harmony.
Releasing pleasure, redolently stated
defining a soulful tranquility.

Suddenly silence, every note muted.
Bravos, shouted, ending a song of love.

LIVING BY CHOICE

What makes us want to live forever,
aging takes a toll on most pleasures?
Reversing life's progress, likely never,
physical change, now takes its measure.

We suffer, yet we want life extended,
to endure a life, for no good reason.
Life was His gift, He chooses to end it,
He knows of a future, with no seasons.

God placed in us, this desire to survive,
limiting ways, to extend our existence.
He knows we love Him, while still alive,
He offers much more, in His presence.

Yet life remains our number one goal,
Small victories, are now so surprising.
Ongoing searches, we seek to unfold,
ending all means, my soul is now rising.

Clearly, my Savoir knows the best way,
to end my foolish, earthly endeavors.
Why should I question His plans today,
completing my joy, with Him forever.

Lift me Lord Jesus, heed not my plea,
the Heavens we love, I now wait to see.

FADING AWAY

Oft I view the wondrous past.
How sweet the thoughts of times before.
With joyful memories, first to last,
Of failures, victories and much more.

In passing days, I grow in faith,
In solitude, I know His way.
My mind, my heart, for God I wait,
To share with Him, that glorious day.

My prayers will soon forever be,
face to face, as my Savior speaks
Reverent, soulful, on my knee,
my faith confirmed, my joy complete.

In His holy presence, I will rejoice,
The precious moment, I hear His voice.

WAVES

Behold the wonders of English language,
one word with so many useful meanings.
Waves have unique purposes in our lives;
beauty, feeling, creating many sounds.

Each wave has a defining existence.
Differences so great, makes one wonder,
about the choices this word describes.

Ocean waves may be a cause of drowning.
water provides a life giving liquid,

. Hair can be shiny with beautiful waves;
waves are also a form of friends greetings.

The sound of musical waves creates joy;·
sound waves of a trains whistle is mournful

Radio waves? unseen? but clearly heard,
sending words through a radio~ speaker.

Magnetic waves supports medical science;
magnets are also used by mechanics.

Knowing these waves? will not make us smart
but using these waves? always sets things apart.

PERSEVERANCE

Do we sometimes, avoid persevering,
When we see, difficult events take place.
Life is simple, when one isn't hearing,
The many things that would slow down our pace.

Tomorrow is always, one day away,
So what if some things, seems bad in our sight.
What value is gained, when we look astray,
While conscience tells us to seek what is right.

Caring for others, is always god's plan,
To fix unfairness, should be our passion.
Neglecting problems, is like shifting sand,
Resolving leads, to stable correction.

God's wisdom, can make things so very clear,
We must always, find ways to persevere.

LIFE SO ENDOWED

Remember when I recalled with delight,
when my mind stirred thoughts of joyful editions.
My youth lacking humility, foresight,
my live so endowed with delightful conditions.

Then I could see how my lacking of reason,
looking ahead as the years rolled by,
led to a number of meaningless seasons,
my values evolving, as harder I tried.

Measuring up to great expectation,
time has passed, later years are present
Loved ones believed my solid foundation,
memories were sweet, so often pleasant.

I now delight in sweet Jesus, my friend,
life everlasting, He gave endurance.
He promised He would meet me at the end,
as a faithful believer, He offered assurance.

Wonderful thoughts, no longer ahead,
new life upon me, like nothing I've led.

TIME

Time is the greatest gift of all indeed,
unseen, never heard, always there to learn.
Used thoughtfully, it meets our every need.
Time passes, not ever to be returned,

God's priceless time, it is ours to obey,
carelessly using it, has no meaning.
Faithful time spent, succeeding each day,
defining value, a pleasant feeling.

God gave all, an equal amount of time,
for faithful use, in His inerrant plan.
Departures from His plan, too many find,
their selfish deeds, have no value for man.

Following God's way, brings all joy and peace,
our world can be, His precious masterpiece.

FAITH

What is faith, how do we find it useful.
is it measurable?, valuable?
It's available to all who want it,
a word with precious meaning and value.

"Faith is the substance of things hoped for,
and evidence of things not seen", Heb.11:1 NKJV
Lives are changed when belief reaches the door,
and faith opens that door revealing the Son.

FRIENDSHIPS

So many friendships, enjoyed in my youth,
sharing life's pleasures, good times together.
Strong ties with dear friends, was absolute proof,
that sweet memories binds us forever.

Making new friends, so simple when younger,
without any cares, each one I cherished.
Then growing old, I had time to wonder,
will new friends be found before I perish?

In later years, some close friends I loved,
emotions so sad, when saying goodbye.
Giving up old friends, most going above,
searching sweet memories, often I cried.

Learning life's lessons, so priceless and true,
making friends when young, the best thing to do.

A MESSAGE FROM GOD

Worshiping god, when we enter his throne,
A message comes clear, some effectual way.
An event takes place, we have never known,
Seeking our heart, we are creatures of clay.

Reverently receiving gracious love,
Often our minds wander, from his presence.
When his precious words, arrive from above,
remember, his forever omniscience.

Reminders of, his eternal caring,
Returns our minds, to our religious past.
Telling him, we will always be sharing,
His will in our lives, must forever last.

Having a faithfulness, full of our love,
Assures great friendship, with our god above.

Psalm 23:1-2 NKJV
The Lord is My Shepherd
I shall not want
He makes me lie down in green pastures
Psalm 23:3-4 NIV
He leads me beside the still waters
He refreshes my soul
He guides me along the right paths for his namesake
Even though I walk through the darkest valley
I will fear no evil for You are with me
Your rod and staff will comfort me
Psalm 23:5 NKJV
You prepare a table before me
In the presence of my enemies
You anoint my head with oil
My cup runs over
Psalm 23:6 BSB
Surely goodness and mercy will follow me all the days of my life
I will dwell in the house of the Lord forever

WHAT IT MEANS TO ME

Jesus is the leader of all my life
He is my provider in all my needs
Jesus provides all the pleasures of life

He is the source of peace in my life

He removes all doubts from my mind
He provides direction in all I do

Life is not always the way we want it
To be

I must trust Him in all situations

He is always prepared for my needs
You show me the truth of your love
In all places and events you are there
I am sanctified by your love

My life is filled abundantly
My future is secure in Your presence
My anticipation of our in-person relationship is
incomprehensible

BLESSINGS

Often we search for God's wisdom in life,
we've heard of his coming, one glorious day.
Seeking God's blessing, as always we strive,
to live like His Son, who showed us the way.

Always remember, He came as a babe,
great joy is knowing, we have his favor.
God's plan for His life, so many to save,
willing to heed, we should never waver.

Using our knowledge, to speak about Him,
believing leads us, to do something nice.
Rewards come after, confessing our sins,
His presence leads us, to a joy filled life.

Receiving His blessing, we have been told,
will capture our hearts, and save our lost souls.

OUR WONDERFUL WORLD

Lives are changed by leaders we have known.
Strong leaders teach, life is always a quest.
Most share knowledge, we often have shown.
Some leaders teaching of God, always best.

What a wonderful world, God's creation,
knowing we have His true love forever.
Sharing our joy and sometimes elation,
every day we can seek new endeavors.

Hearing of God's love is always so good,
finding His truths of which there are many
Learning his Word, not always understood.
life is worth living, truths there are plenty.

Releasing passions for our God alone,
expecting to know Him when we go home.

REVIVAL, A SONNET

Exploring a way to worship His name,
with regard to the precious tenets read.
Seeking wisdom, from lives already claimed,
explaining desires, and cares being said.

A meeting for fellowship, with one's peer,
beginning with prayers, to share with their God.
Soulful music evokes feeling so clear,
tears of joy reaching, where man does not trod.

Loud voices, sending a message of joy,
to a Savior devine, in Heaven so near.
Organ, viola, sweet sounds to employ
worship resounds for all voices to hear.

Revivals create wonderful emotions
where all can recite love and devotion.

MY PRAYER

Heavenly Father
You know all my weaknesses,
my weakness reveals Your strength.
You know all my foolish desires,
your wisdom replaces these cares.
My temptations overwhelm me,
You replace them, with strength and faith.
Make my faith complete in all things.
Teach me, by holding me accountable.
Lead me in right living, for Your sake.
Remind me always, of Your Commands.
Forgive me, for all unforgiven sins.
When I am weak, strengthen my faith.
In You Christ, all things are possible
This is my personal prayer.
AMEN

LIFE SO AMAZING

Remember when I recalled with delight,
when my mind stirred thoughts of joyful editions.
My youth lacking humility, foresight,
my live so treated with delightful conditions

Then I could see how my lacking of reason,
looking ahead as the years rolled by
led to a number of meaningless seasons
my values evolving as harder I tried.

To measure up to great expectation,
time is passing, latter years are present
Loved ones believe my solid foundation
memories were sweet, so often pleasant

Now I delight in sweet Jesus, my friend
for life everlasting, God gave assurance
He promised we would meet at the end
as a faithful believer, He offers endurance

A wonderful thought such as this lies ahead
New life unending, like nothing I've led

A GIFT FROM GOD

Life is a wonderful gift, from our God,
through Him, we experience great pleasures.
Meaningful good things, we never find odd,
others we struggle, to create new measures.

Of happiness, love, other refinements,
passions can rise up, to lead us astray.
Some things we find, need careful assignment,
God's gifts provide, a real motive each day.

To reach out to friends, who may be in need,
searching to determine, things to provide.
Lending support, is a blessing indeed,
knowing He is always, there at our side.

He never fails, to deliver this word,
life is precious, we so clearly have heard.

MY LEGACY

I leave a legacy, others will see,
it's all that remains, it must stand alone.
Friends will discuss, that's okay with me,
it's no longer my choice, how well it was done.

Some will remember, dislike or enjoy,
sharing past pleasures, sadness or success.
Emotions evolved, from memories employed,
tears were wiped out, as mistakes were confessed.

God's presence was evident, this I pray;
He was my leader, as I sought His Name.
He stood by my side, many times each day,
whatever happened, I accepted the blame.

My life as revealed, in my legacy,
hopefully the best of me, all will see.

DREAMS

Most dreams, are wonderfully confusing,
many of which, can be very exciting,
fooling our minds, though not of our choosing,
leading to simple ways, of delighting.

Bad dreams are often, not very pleasant,
many dreams frequently, seem like a play,
leading our subconscious, far from the present,
to fantasy land, where we cannot stay.

Scary dreams, are rightly called nightmares,
living a bad dream, can wake us up early.
Dreaming of traveling, not knowing where,
rudely awakened, can make one surly.

Sweet dreams, can lead us to comforting sleep,
but wake us often, with our dreams incomplete.

WINDOWS

So good to look through my window each day,
trees, birds, weather much beauty to see.
My life passes by quietly knowing today,
windows reveal the great outdoors for me.

My isolation from outdoors provides,
few ways to observe all things in the sun.
Seeing others as if I am hiding,
watching my friends through the window is fun.

Without windows the world would pass me by,
only to look at pictures on the wall.
Not seeing the outdoors would make me cry,
with windows, thank God, I can see it all.

Observing accidents leaves me so sad,
wondering if someone is badly hurt.
Praying to God, not knowing, but glad,
by knowing His love will never desert.

Seeing, not hearing, is often so strange,
what they are saying leaves me to wonder.
Sadly I can't hear as I'm out of range,
weird thoughts occur like a cloud I'm under.

My great joy at seeing God's world today,
without windows life would wither away.

SPORTS

A GOLF SONNET

Golf, not a game for the timid of mind,
some awesome challenges rattle the brain.
So many situations one will find,
to make them wish they would get a hard rain.

A players performance, sometimes is bad,
big drivers put fear in opponents hearts.
Dropping long curling putts, takes up the slack,
Short irons a sure way to set them apart.

A gentleman's sport a pleasure to see,
The few that cheat bring disgrace to the game.
Good golfers follow the rules to a tee,
Some fail to see how their cheating brings shame.

Real golfers have learned such profound respect,
They protect the game for those who come next.

FOOTBALL

A game to exhibit great muscle and speed,
more than a show, it's a time to compete
Fierce struggles required to ever succeed,
ends only when one foe concedes defeat.

Worthy the player who honors his foe,
Game plans, strategies all designed to win.
Skills and great feats, more than a show,
Each combined to gain victory at the end.

What is it that makes football so much fun?
strong runners, true passes, fumbles so bad.
Until the game ends we'll not know who won,
Losers will ask was that really fun they had?

We second guess a game plan if they lose,
and take credit for ones that led to a win.
The game result always leads us to choose,
that a football game is fun 'til the end.

TRAVELING

Most traveling can be good for the soul,
walking, driving, flying ever revealing,
observing life and landscape our goal,
nature and people there for our seeing.

Most, we observe embracing a lifestyle,
enjoying events in moments so measured.
So often our viewing producing a smile,
searching the roads, for a visual pleasure.

Capturing a scene so full of intrigue,
our senses expand to fully remind,
of life's many simple ways, to succeed,
searching the by ways, enjoying our time.

Expanding our knowledge, of time and place,
Enjoying God's sweet gift of life and space.

ALL SPORTS ARE FUN

Sports, a good part of life, all can enjoy,
a home run, a touchdown a three point shot.
Though so many years, since I was a boy,
thrills, I still feel, though a player I'm not.

Skills body, muscle, and mind all in play,
with good fellowship, the thrill to compete.
To win subline, but the game is the way,
both players and fans, share joy of the meet.

The team that wins, a moment of elation,
losing finds solace, in good play and rest.
Ending there comes, a period of reflection,
though not winning, they played their very best.

Sure of the future, their time will soon come.
Tables will turn, that's why sports are such fun.

TROPHIES

Fulfilling a goal never suspected,
A lifetime of effort at last achieved.
Feeling so blessed by being selected,
Dreams are discovered, so hard to believe

A work of beauty for many to see.
Envied by some who will always desire,
fame for a talent that doesn't come free.
Honors accepted from those we admire.

Crowds applauding at the presentation,
admired by all those who love the winner.
Approved by thousands across the Nation,
inspires a challenge for young beginners

Final completion, an honor, long sought,
God blesses talent, it can never be bought.

FOOD

Who will admit to a food addiction?
Some will admit to a phase for a while.
Health nuts will always claim it's not fiction,
they exist in a state of denial.

Kids hate spinach, later it's cauliflower,
others love peas, but beans are rejected.
Diet foods chosen, not often devoured,
favorite foods are always selected.

Diets are used to manage health issues
and often designed to control the waist.
Some women choose to look like a tissue,
starving themselves, clearly lacking good taste.

God gave good foods in abundance to eat,
we thank Him daily for bread, milk and meat.

FISHING

A pass time that is always a pleasure,
to feel the tug on a line brings a thrill.
Hoping it is a fish, too big to measure,
happy to catch one, my bucket to fill.

Going for a big one, heading out to sea,
traveling far with great expectations.
Exciting to wonder how big it could be,
the thrill of the ride causing elation.

Waves rolling the boat side to side,
i'm feeling nausea building in me.
Slowly weakening, hard as I tried,
to be a seaman, but wanting to flee.

Suddenly, the dreaded event took place,
over the side, I lost all that was in me.
Weakened, embarrassed, I clearly lost face,
my stomach lurched, and then I was free.

Back to my fishing gear, taking my place,
waiting for action I knew would occur.
My tackle prepared for a serious race,
it begins to make a tremendous whirr.

The tug on my rod I've been waiting for,
caused my heart to leap, my nerves to tremble.
Reeling so hard, I could not ask for more,
that hard pull I will always remember.

Finally he surfaced, man what a sight,
he never weakened, not giving an inch
He jumped and dove putting on a great fight.
Reeling him in was not really a cinch.

I tired and began to have second thoughts.
This fish had a great desire to survive.
Against impossible odds, he has fought,
I am feeling, he should remain alive.

With feelings of reverence, I cut the line
releasing this powerful sea warrior.
A surge of relief and sadness defined,
my action, to me, remains no failure.

INVESTMENTS, A SONNET

A word with many uses, and meanings,
causing joy, sadness, often frustration.
Investments can cause, many kinds of feelings,
ranging from anger, to great elation.

Investments of love for a mother's child,
revealing emotions, for time well spent.
Artistic investments, not always mild,
exposes skills, in compelling events.

Finding the Lord, our greatest investment,
His example revealed the greatest love.
Passion, defined by His lonely statement,
the cross, His gift, from His Father above.

Ignoring His love, a great oversight,
embracing His teaching is always right.

HISTORY

A STORY OF VALOR

A story of valor often told
Men of the Alamo serving that day
Heard many words of an enemy bold
Approaching with clear intent to stay

Leaving was not an option or reason
Fighting for freedom with only one thought
Ready to die, should this be the season
Clashing of wills, a battle to be fought

Hours of waiting, so agonizing
Visions of certain death, weighed on the mind
Weapons of battle quickly arriving
Preparing to die for those left behind

Dawn came on early, surprisingly bright
Exposing hordes for battle on the way
Weapons now firing in the glare of light
Heroes will die on this memorable day

Stinging red spots on a warriors chest
Bayonets flashing as bodies meet
Blood shooting from a soldiers vest
Giving no quarter no thought of defeat

Men with guns blazing with bodies so near
Cannonballs crashing destroying their nests
Cheering each other to manage their fear
Standing to die fighting Santa Anna's best

Sweat and blood, given without remorse
Destiny has fallen on a few brave men
Will history recall this battle's course
Silence revealing the ultimate end

Common men's lives defining our fate
For peace and a lasting independence
Providing the future for a rising state
Texans all know why this battle made sense.

REPRISE

After the sickening Alamo fight
Civilians fleeing their oncoming fate
Enemy forces showing their might
A great leader appeared, and not too late

Promised victory in a time not far
Choosing the right time to show the way
The small army was assembled for war
A surprise attack was not far away

Finding the enemy, too tired to know
Sleeping, resting before their next conquest
Suddenly, "Remember the Alamo"
Rang loudly in their ears, ending their rest

Surprised and overwhelmed were they
Enemy warriors, brought to swift defeat
No match for the small army's way
Defeat of the enemy army complete

Leaders met to bring the war to an end
A treaty was signed, let peace be the norm
Success for an army of uncommon men
The Great State of Texas now will be formed.

EVERY DAY HEROES

Who are these people who live in danger,
saving many lives is their one passion.
With no concern for themselves, nor anger,
serving for many, for others, their mission.

We know them as son, neighbor or friend,
they work as our brothers, they care.
Treacherous places they must enter in,
bad places where most would not even dare.

A special part in our great nation's might,
we honor them as patriots with praise.
Saving a soldier in a bloody fight,
flag of our nation, proudly we raised.

Facing near death in a fire ravaged store,
knowing many lives are in jeopardy.
Using their axes, firemen search for more,
in danger, resisting the urge to flee.

The seas rolling waves in stormy weather,
creating dangerous, swift undertows.

Swimmers, enjoying great fun together,
ignoring danger the lifeguard knows.

Attacking the powerful frothing waves,
he saves from drowning the weakest one first.
He rescues others, he struggles to save,
with his own lungs almost ready to burst.

Today, we also are proud of our medics,
who face a deadly, contagious disease.
They have no choice, but follow our edicts,
caring for sick lives, working hard to please.

All mighty warriors live life on an edge,
Their faith in God keeps them always steady.
We promise with prayer to sustain our pledge,
the Savior's hand, is forever ready

THE STORM NAMED HARVEY

Many bad storms, in my lifetime I've seen,
nothing compared, to a storm named Harvey.
Hurricane, rainfall leaving major destruction.

We borrowed a friend's, second floor bedroom.
When morning arrived, with an earie silence,
we were shocked, to see massive destruction.

Harvey's deep waters covered our homes,
our furnishings, our cars, nothing remained.
We never imagined, such total destruction.

From raging overnight rains, and the rivers,
leaving their powerful, statement of doom.
Our hearts fell, when we saw the destruction.

It seemed like an end, to a good generation,
with no promise ever, of possible recovery.
Yet we knew, we had to fix the destruction.

Contractors met, with we saddened owners,
of homes so clearly, requiring restoration,
to replace basic needs, gone by destruction.

Stores and salespersons, usually sympathetic;
they also knew they could offer assistance,
with product values, clearly set post destruction.

We did take pleasure, in restoring our home,
with all new and creative, artistic designs,
for a home left empty, by total destruction

Now fully restored, new, better than before,
but so many treasures, never to be recovered,
lost forever, Harvey's unforgiving destruction.

HIS TOWN

Living in the heart of an area in decay
where many have no hope for a future.
Their lives were focused on living each day,
not searching for higher forms of culture.

At meal time, prayers of sincere thanks to God
for meager servings of tasteless cold bread.
Bedtime, after prayers, so easy to nod,
sleeping, not easy on hard lumpy beds.

Morning light filters through cracks in the wall,
starting a new day, not much to savor.
Black coffee, stale toast or nothing at all,
work at the mill, a day of hard labor.

Why is his life so miserable today,
he's fully committed to live for Christ?
His rewards will be in Heaven they say,
a little help now, would be very nice.

His country provides the pathway to peace,
freedom to live the best life that he can.
No law keeps him from living as he seeks,
his life is free of all dictated plans.

Some day he will find that dreamed of success,
learning new skills lead to certain progress.
God and his country delivers the rest,
making ways to find a good life, so blessed.

THIS OLD HOUSE

A wonderful place, where I was born,
many great years, of our history it stored.
Built to last, it survived many storms.
Memories remain, we were never bored.

The long front porch, was used every day,
friendly neighbors, passing by stopped to talk.
Many loved ones, often enjoyed their stay,
strangers stopped by, during an evening walk.

A big fireplace, our only source of heat.
Wood framed windows, leaking cold winter air,
open for summer breezes, always so sweet.
frequent bad weather, but under God's care.

A giant sycamore tree, shared the side view,
flowers gave beauty, the old house needed.
Ivy covered walls, made nothing look new,
rooftop leaves, left the old view completed.

Warm evenings gave us, great outdoor shows.
Scratchy old radio, best we could buy,
Jack Armstrong, Green Hornet,
The Shadow knows.
Throwing at bats, as dusk darkened the sky.

Master bath was a round, galvanized tub,
No shower yet designed, to meet our needs.
Time wasted, cleaning me with loving rubs,
always to satisfy, sweet mother's pleas.

Our lives now, has so clearly been changed,
the one I preferred, was surely the best.
The old days, in my view, were better arranged,
my old house remembered, as a nice nest.

The old house, no longer is there today,
great memories will never go away.

TRAMPS

Men who have lost their way,
asking nothing, nothing to say.
Without a friend to care

No cause to seek, or thought to own,
within their minds no seeds are sown.
Without a friend to care

A good mind, always at rest,
finding never that which is best.
Without a friend to care

Failing to have a sense of pride,
unwilling to improve never tried.
Without a friend to care

Lacking motives to gain life's needs,
not even a desire or time to read.
Without a friend to care

It's clear our God knows this man.
Some day He will show that he can.
Without a friend to care

With God he now finds simple ways,
to occupy his lonely days.
Without a friend to care

He found a small dog all alone,
it had no home to call it's own.
He found a friend to care

Now giving as one forgiven,
he loved the gift God had given.
He's now the friend who cares.

REPRISE

It's difficult to survive on the street,
and even provide food for his dog to eat.
God's Love is always there

Knowing they live alone on the dole,
Sometimes their life touches a soul.
God's Love is always there

A generous man one day walked by;
he said, I could help if you would try.
God's Love is always there

The man offered to provide some work,
the tramp said I will, no job will I shirk.
God's Love is always there

A job, a home, a new way of life;
friends, relatives maybe someday a wife.
God's Love is always there

The little dog God must have sent,
now has a home and is very content.
God's Love is always there

COMMUTING

A daily Long Island railroad commute,
was always a challenge to my patience.
Hope for safe arrival on a bad route,
Into a wild Manhattan confluence.

Winter commutes bring even more misery,
in antique trains we travel to our work.
Broken windows in ten degree weather,
no source providing heat of any sort.

Sitting close to a large, total stranger;
badly needed warmth, but often scented.
Miles of a rough, noisy ride in our anger,
disturbing views, of miles of tenements.

Folks who were born here did not seem to mind,
I wonder why I endure such travel.
A peaceful trip, I'm not likely to find,
without this commute, life would unravel.

After years of praying, God heard my plea,
wonderful new commuter cars were built.
My travel to work suddenly seemed free,
anger and distress, there was no more guilt.

Thank you Lord that my whole life changed,
my work attitude so greatly improved.
At work and at home, my life rearranged,
Good times with life, where my God rules.

Commuting by train, can take its measure,
it took our God to make it a pleasure.

WISDOM

WISDOM

An attribute never easy to find,
claimed by many, not all valid choices,
a conditional mental state of mind,
seldom revealed by very loud voices.

Able to analyze most complex ideas,
searching answers, not obvious to all.
Willing ventures to new thoughts without fear,
never concerned, always willing to fall.

A distinctive view of many events,
seeking new ways, not obvious to most,
to understand one our gracious God sent.
Talent revealed from our Heavenly Host.

Wisdom understands people's afflictions,
reasons for friendships, relatonships, love.
Wisdom to separate truth from fiction,
Including reasons for gifts from above.

Many disruptions are left undefined,
seeking God's wisdom, accepting His ways,
we acknowledge with clarity his designs.
With discernment it's clear what He has to say.

Moments of silence and a peaceful mind,
conditions that promise wisdom's presence.
The Bible makes answers, not hard to find,
with God's perfect love, and His omniscience.

WORDS

The magnificence of God's gift to man
With which humans express their emotions
Voices explain current events at hand
Language reveals all types of promotions

A simple statement taken for granted
Yet lacking voices our thoughts live alone
Speaking can lead to ideas well planted
Revealing our thoughts, so much can be shown

Listening for words that makes impressions
Hearing is better than all we can say
Unless we seek to leave an expression
Providing a message just for the day

While speaking can be very enlightening
Listening to speech can become boring
Loud voices can sometimes be frightening
But without words, there's no love outpouring

Since Jesus hears all our voices clearly
By His words we learn to love Him dearly

MOMENTS

There is a key point in every event
Involving a certain time and a place
Lives are changed without known intent

A moment of error can change one's life
With little time to measure an action
Conditions so quickly lead to real strife

Memory can't repeat what just took place
Instinctive acts might prevent disaster
A moment in time causes minds to race

one moment can even cause real laughter
We will never know what God plans next
Some moments we can remember after

Serious moments we hope to retain
To keep from going completely insane

DECISIONS

Making decisions, a place in your house,
Choices, Options are always available.
Living in difficult times with your spouse,
Some choices, not always on the table.

Silence may be the only safe action,
to make certain, we avoid a crisis.
Harsh comments, can lead to bad reactions,
it's always best, to be at your nicest.

Sometimes, it's impossible to agree,
Discussion never reveals, who is right.
Silence, is always best to remain free,
of insults and anger, throughout the night.

When answers appear, from Heaven above
Acknowledge the source, and heed the advice.
Restore good fellowship, with sincere love,
Forgetting conflicts, it's time to be nice.

Restoring real trust, our sincere desire,
to hear God's perfect word, always inspires.

PROMISES

A word defined with so many choices;
nouns of value, we share with our voices.

Verbs of so many serious meanings,
words of deception, to hide real feelings.

A promise all cherish, very good health,
some chose a promise of very great wealth.

A promise of love reveals emotions,
of passion or joy, when set in motion.

Political pundits promise the truth,
believing themselves, hoping you do too.

Firemen promise to douse every flame,
saving victims, not knowing their names.

Policeman's promise, you're under arrest,
they'll take you to jail unless you confess.

The doctor's promise of healing is sweet,
we hope his diagnosis is complete.

Business contracts promise very big deals,
read the fine print, some text may be unreal.

Religious preachers promise God's blessings,
all that's required, is sincere confessing.

PATIENCE

An attribute shared by all who want it,
to have in reserve, when things go wrong.
Avoiding conflicts, as a daily habit,
greeting a problem, which should not last long.

We once knew an old lady named Patience,
who loved and cared for the sick and the lame.
A best friend, one who would always pray for,
and handle a conflict, as if only a game.

My crippled grandmother loved old Patience,.
she came each day to encourage her friend.
A diabetic, granny still had good sense,
to realize how good old Patience had been.

As a child, I looked forward to her visits,
excited to see what old Patience had.
she brought us goodies, and other tidbits,
my brother and I were always so glad.

She was a tall, slender, black lady and poor,
when blacks were not respected by many.
But, with a generous heart, and much more,
the love she offered, was more than plenty.

A long time passed, Old Patience stopped coming,
Granny waited patiently for her visit.
One day, a young boy passed by our home,
I asked about Old Patience, he hesitated,

My grandmother, has gone on to heaven,
he sobbed, as he was only eleven.

TOMORROW

What about tomorrow, that makes any sense?
foresight will usually, lead to success.
To know nothing sure, leaves one in suspense,
doing mindless things, often leave a mess.

Tomorrow could come, a time to rejoice,
our conscious minds, His existence so real.
God's presence revealed, when we hear his voice,
we hope tomorrow, the way that we feel.

Believing closeness comes, when we remain,
ready to worship, our Lord's sweet refrains.
Tomorrow might bring, hardship and sorrow,
God's help is real, today and tomorrow.

When we faithfully reveal, our true needs,
He's present tomorrow, all things He heeds.

CRYING

Why is it natural, that children cry?
They cry when, by accident, they are hurt.
Many things happen, they do not know why,
like when not allowed, to play in the dirt.

Adults cry also, but what brings our tears?
We cry when bad things, cause our hearts distress.
Or we learn of sad things in coming years,
though we grow older, our hearts cry no less.

Our emotions, God's way leading to prayer,
crying is certain, when loved ones are lost.
God touches our souls, just showing He cares,
His loving concern, reduces our cost

He's always there, as we reveal our fears,
It's His way to comfort, our later years.

MR. BURROWS

He erased the blackboard
after describing an example
of the Pythagorean theorem.
He made math sound so simple.

Some listened, I and others whispered
Young minds were wandering.
An eraser thrown, was retrieved
on a young students head.

Mr. Burrows spoke calmly, as he said,
answer this question young man,
you, who hit her on the head.
Describe for me this isosceles triangle.

Such was school days, before I went away
Time passed,
now in college, working hard to make an A.

Freshman visits by my High school teachers
was going to be a tale to be told.
As I, the bad boy in high school,
had made the freshman honor roll.

Mr. Burrows and my Principal
Sat at a desk in a college hall,
Hearing excuses for bad grades.
My Army time, was not wasted at all.

My name was on the honor roll.
Mr. Burrows and my Principal laughed.
I could not be the bad boy who
played all through high school.

Making c- on most required subjects.
My high school fun was now over
Now a plaque in my honor,
hangs where I once had fun.

Making a statement under the sun
showing how having some fun,
can be followed by hard work,
accomplishing much.

NUMBERS

Who can know the big numbers we live by?
to measure the number of breaths we take.
Thousands each day, we cannot even try,
and count the frequent, small steps that we make.

Or see flocks of birds, soaring in the sky,
counting numbers, can bring clairification.
Autos so numerous, passing us by,
for those who need, more frustration.

Its better we seek, other green pastures,
the only way, to retain our good sense.
Limiting mindless, searching for measures,
closing our eyes, we do try to condense.

Life's major events, to simple confession,
that big numbers, are only expressions.

ANTICIPATION

A five syllable word, with so many uses,
in our worries, it is the first thing we do.
Words which often, reveal our excuses,
hoping what happens will surely come true.

We anticipate good, in all events,
without full knowledge of the future.
We create thoughts, of possible intent,
satisfied to wait, is not in our nature.

Songs have been written, using the word;
true love or passion, is often the theme.
Visions inspire, to believe what is heard,
great pleasures imagined, as we dream.

Failure to trust, in God's intervention,
leaves only, fleeting anticipation.

DOUBTING

Why does one doubt the freedoms we enjoy,
when we can plainly see the moon and stars.
Seeking all measures of tasks to employ,
while making our choice of multiple cars.

Are there any doubts, when we seek a mate,
no problem, we can always be ready,
to sweep up our choice before it's too late.
Nothing requires, we have to go steady.

On the dance floor with a neat boy I knew,
Weaving and twirling, the dance incomplete,
I had no doubt, he would step on my shoe.
Handsome but, uncertain about his feet.

Singing is something we have doubts about,
Raising our voice like a high soprano,
The noise came out much like a friendly shout.
There was no doubt, my singing had to go.

There must be things we have no doubt about,
we'll never know for sure, without any doubt.

YESTERDAY

Something about yesterday was troubling to me,
events about which I cared.

Reviewing each minute I could undeniably see,
another day full of snares.

Recalling meaningless things that took place,
causing my worries today.

Events which mysteriously led me to embrace,
messages I've felt God say.

Sharing with Jesus always stills my heart,
when I reveal it all.

God's pure message, to my mind imparts,
magical thoughts to recall.

His simple words provide pure realizations,
revealing how little I know.

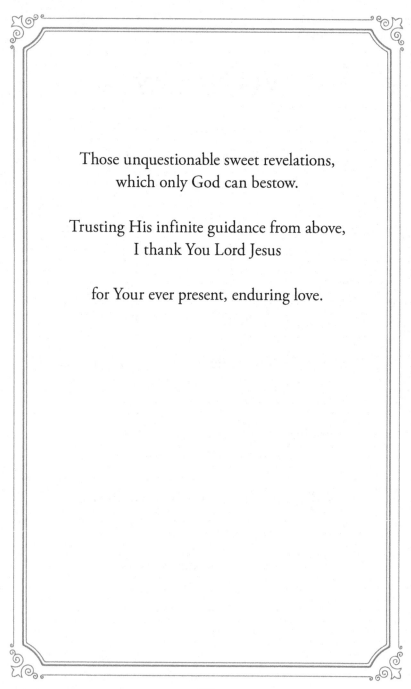

Those unquestionable sweet revelations,
which only God can bestow.

Trusting His infinite guidance from above,
I thank You Lord Jesus

for Your ever present, enduring love.

MUSIC

Can there be sounds, so very pure and sweet,
rhythms that sometimes mixes with voices.
Contemporary links that strangely meet;
they seem to be, just synchronized noises.

Vision of images, often delighting,
pleasant versions, which we clearly enjoy.
Leading to passions often exciting,
sounds promoting and expanding our joy.

Joining harsh metals, with soft waving winds,
creating pure notes, heralding such greatness.
Leading your senses to absorb fine blends,
producing sound, so clear without loudness

Bringing to focus, great beautiful sound,
Wonders of music so many have found.

BOOKS

Wonders can be revealed in a good book
Adventures excite the mind as we read
Sadness can overcome one so easily
Feeling the writers instincts indeed

Tasting the fervor of the books dealings
Reaching the climax leads to emotions
Joy, sadness or incomplete feelings
Messages echoes through our minds

They do so without showing mercy
Waiting for the meaning to be complete
Knowing how much the message leaves
Wishing we knew why some things happen

Knowing it is only fiction doesn't matter
Real messages clear our confusion
Certain of our ideas about the ending
Not wanting, fearing, the final conclusion

Reaching a pinnacle of joy in the reading
Forgetting it is not going to happen
Does not change the anxious pleadings
Looking back we see the reasons

Forward thinking will lead us away
Best stay with the author's intentions
Changing the outcome is often pleasing
Searching for answers which are not fair

Listening for measures which are not there
Watching for signs of revisions worth seeing
Fantasy worlds can be so clearly lending
To a real life condition with clear meaning

Messages echo wildly through our minds,
searching for meaningful revelations.
Creating useful, thought provoking lines,
happening without clear explanation.

Knowing it's fiction is of no concern.
Adventurous stories excite our dreams,
Measures of pleasures often not earned,
Forgetting it's really not as it seems

Changing the outcome is often pleasing,
but staying with the author's conclusions,
leaves one certain we have a good ending.
A real life story with no wild delusions.

Revealing the answers at the book's end
Meaningful messages to tell my friends
Ending the story the writer intended
Leaves one so certain we have a better

Ending.

POLITICS

POLITICS

Matters of state have politics involved
One party thinks they control the debate
Partisan problems are there to be solved
They call for the vote before it's too late

Bad Speeches come as others endeavor
Filibusters so frequently take place
To make stalling tactics last forever
Defeat the losers not willing to face

Bad members complain when facing defeat
The winners take their victory and say
Whining about voting they cannot beat
To all voters, you must extend my stay

Undisclosed cost of their popular win
Taxpayers always pay in the end

AMERICA

A Nation alive

Formed by God-fearing men
Designed to survive

Strengthened by one simple trend
All men are equal

On a gracious God we depend
Joined by a joyful men.

Love and respect for all mankind
With fully expressed

Ways to serve God's precious design
Our nation, so blessed

Freedom, our most sacred trust
Loving our destiny

Our motto, In God we Trust

HARD TIMES

This is a sad time for our country today.
In any national or worldwide crises,
our country has always pulled together,
winning battles, wars and epidemics.

Patriotism at those times, at its greatest,
political beliefs, were of minor concern.
Two parties, unified for the battle,
sharing, fighting, meeting the call to arms.

Corona Virus has consumed our nation.
One political party will not join the fight,
consumed with partisanship, in the crisis,
selfish control of lives, more important.

Our government leaders, are overworked,
striving to ease, the public's dilemma.
Searching, for a medical solution,
anything soon, not really be expected.

Answers from our God, will come,
when He is ready, to show us the ways.
Anti-dotes found, relieving the illness,
fully healing, the worldwide Pandemic.

Restoring the old ways, to live our lives,
praying each day, to receive His blessings.
No longer neglecting, our hours of worship,
recognizing again, our God is forgiving.

Seeking His will, always sows the seeds,
for meeting all of mankind's true needs.

MILLENNIALS

Our future leaders, the youth of today,
refusing to learn from established norms.
Lacking concern about history's way,
failing to care how our Nation was formed.

Radical teachers ignoring the past,
leading innocent minds planting the seeds.
Promoting a way that cannot last,
stating our country is twisted by greed.

Opposite thoughts are never permitted,
refusing to hear history's real evidence.
Filled with hatred, minds fully committed
to failed governments that never made sense

Ignoring Capitalism's successes,
false teaching to change hearts of our youth.
Hoping to cause our nation to regress,
promoting socialist views as if truth.

With no knowledge of real consequences,
filled with false visions of national bliss.
Millennial follow paths so senseless,
unwilling to hear truth, facts clearly missed

Wisdom of our founders is very strong
in the hearts of real patriots today.
The message of socialism is wrong,
and will be erased by freedoms' great way

God Bless America, freedom will stand,
false doctrines will never control this land.

PASSING BY

Where are those decades, that have passed us by?
Did history, not leave a mark on us?
Young rebels, have a good reason to try,
They often said, time we no longer trust

Many years of our great freedom, enjoyed,
Our forefathers courage, made happiness sure.
Soldiers so often, suddenly employed,
Wars and peace times, hard living, they endured

Drifting of values, we quietly observed,
with lack of concern, for their fellow man.
Highest self regard, the thing they most served,
new beginnings without much of a plan.

Warnings of failure, from pundits galore,
not heeding advice, from experienced men.
Struggles to exist. as free men no more.
expecting disaster. the message they send.

Their way of leading, cannot survive long,
Many times tried, all efforts failed to last.
Leaders gained power. to do what is wrong,
Forgetting the truth. of the recent past.

Elections assure, that good laws are saved
Socialism cannot. survive in this nation,
land of the free, and home of the brave.
Liberal laws, can't meet expectations.

By Ten Commandments, our laws were formed,
drawn to ensure, human's freedom intent.
Centuries have shown, it remains the norm,
refined by our Constitution, all God sent.

THE RADICAL LEFT

Our country's under siege, from an evil so strong,
desperate for power, they have ruthless intent.
History has revealed, that such rebellion is wrong,
resorting to foul lies, and evil plots with contempt.
Beware of the Socialist State

An evil ideology Socialism, destroys all fair play,
by silencing excellence, and freedom of thought.
Weakening our leaders, losing faith in our way,
ruthless acts, deceit, things we've always fought.
Beware of the Radical Left

Revealing our contempt, for their gutless disdain,
strong leaders, laws and patriotism, brings light.
With strength and determination, it's very plain,
evidence that good people, are willing to fight.
Beware of Liberal Schemes

Anger and pride, our weapons against rebellion,
over all fear, hate, hypocrisy, and evil domains.
Our nation's traditions, are not for cruel dissection,
and not to be changed, they shall always remain.
Beware of Socialism

Our Lord leads the battle, He's always there,
His guidance reveals, how very much he cares,
Be sure, of the Power of Prayer.

DUPLICITY

A powerful word so often misused,
usually with unpleasant intentions.
A misleading message, a spoken ruse,
hearers are not sure a truth was mentioned.

Tools of politics, always misleading,
expecting to gain a false advantage.
Actual truths, with serious meanings,
mislead by lying, leaves hearers outraged.

Media plots to make messages bad,
duplicity is used, promoting their deed.
Seeing thru their game makes smart people mad,
truth has no value, they only know greed.

Those with integrity will call them out,
since the damage has been done, they care not.
Misleading news is what they are about,
defeating their opponent, their only shot.

The power to report false news today,
led by a dangerous neo Marxist gang.
Destroying freedom, the obvious way,
their evil duplicity, supports the bang.

Good citizens who love their great nation,
are fully aware of dangers ahead.
With patriotic determination,
and God's help such plots, certain to be dead.

Elections will stop all threats such as these,
our votes will support whomever we please.

MR. PRESIDENT,

Today you are living, what everyone dreams;
Character, posture, sure of your actions.
Most have no idea, what the office means,
Willing to hear, some opposite factions.

Always aware, of political junctions,
You lead the nation, with vigorous fire.
Those who oppose, your most valid functions,
Much to the pleasure, of those you admire

Many endeavor, to block out your rules,
When problems arrive you join in the fight.
Fervor and wits, you must have as your tools,
your answers are always, full true and bright.

Receive your help, through god's will you must,
Pray you will guide us, by god's royal trust.

WHY DO I CARE

Anger defines weakness, not ever strength.
Reporters of doom, can often be linked.
Why should I care about this?

Caring does matter, much more than we thought,
Anger restores, many people who fought.
Why should I care about this?

Walls can be hiding, what we should not see.
Hearing suffices, what we have for free.
Why should I care about this?

A secret can be moved from false to true.
Many themes are nice, but some will not do.
Why should I care about this?

Protecting a secret, reveals great trust.
Keeping a secret, for friendships we must.
That's why I care about this!

Winning can always, demand our respect.
Losing, we find many ways to reflect.
Why should I care about this?

Winning a friendship, often is priceless.
Losing leaves time, for life changing success.
That's why I care about this!

Solomon saw nothing, under the sun.
Meaningless measures, he overlooked none.
Yes, I do care about this!

DEATH OF DEMOCRACY

"A Democracy cannot exist as a permanent form of Government. It can only exist until the voters discover that they can vote themselves money from the public treasury. From that moment on the majority always votes for the candidates promising the most money from the public treasury with the result that a Democracy always collapses over loose fiscal policy followed by a Dictatorship.

The average length of the world's greatest civilizations has been 200 years. these nations have gone through the following sequence:

From bondage to spiritual faith;
from spiritual faith to great courage;
from courage to liberty;
from liberty to abundance;
from abundance to selfishness;

from selfishness to complacency;
from complacency to apathy;
from apathy to dependency;
from dependency back to bondage.""

Alexander Tyler, 17th Century,
in the time of the 13 Colonies.

ENDINGS

ENDINGS

Enduring sounds of sweet life apart
Completes the silence of our being
Creating memories to fill my heart
Looking forward to dreams I'm seeing

Wondering when a clear light will shine
Visions of angels soaring above
Placing thoughts in a very old mind
Whispers of messages about God's love

Changing of value, revered by so many
Completing struggles for searching souls
Meaningful signs of infinite plenty
Lonely thoughts prevail and control

Finding solace in places not known
Hearing so many confuses the soul

WHATEVER HAPPENS

Life is so confusing; I have no way to go.
How can I know, where is my future?

Can't I know right, what is right?
What is wrong, who will lead me?
How will I know, when will I go?

Where am I going, life is so confusing.
Will there be a day when I will know?

Does my God hear my plea to know?
Why must I know, whatever happens,
I will know, but why should I know?

Why does it matter, I must do it.
No need to know, it will happen.

It will be done, I didn't know,
I cannot know, what happened?

I will do whatever happens.
I know, it will be soon.

PLACES

Memories about, travels to places,
dear old friends, we encountered, not often.
Enjoying and remembering faces,
sharing good times, many facts were softened.

At times we found, no meaningful way.
Our travels were for, the joy of being,
at places, visits, not for a long stay.
Enjoying places, scenes all worth seeing.

Far from our home, we saw many great sights,
but knowing how great, our pleasure and play,
just made us believe, the trip was done right.
We knew without doubt, that we could not stay.

But our minds were always comforted by,
saving time, for a nice parting goodbye.

END TIMES

Enduring thoughts, of our life now apart,
completes the near silence of my being.
Cauldrons of memories, now fill my heart,
reaching sadly for dreams, not for seeing.

Seeking new values, revered by so many,
not ever struggling, but searching my soul.
for meaningful views of life full of plenty,
lonely thoughts, never prevail or control.

The very moment a clear light will shine,
real visions of angels soaring above,
placing new thoughts, in a stately old mind,
whispering messages, of God's pure love.

Finding a real peace, in a place so pure,
hearing as God, clearly comforts the soul.
Anxiously seeking, a time for closure,
agony replaced, by flashes so bold.

Fears of death, mixed with untimely glee,
joy finds a way, even in our sorrow,
knowing for sure, God is hearing my plea,
tenets of destiny, starting tomorrow.

Sincere remorse, will find no support,
Visions of Heaven, herein to report.

LIFE AND THE HEREAFTER

What is most important to mankind,
Living this life, or meeting with Jesus?
As one grows older, Christ works on our mind,
Our soul and our body, as He prepares us.

One wonders, what such transitions appeal,
Jesus in person, a thought which will stay.
Death seems so cruel, but heaven so real,
Since God is with us already each day.

Why rush to that glorious decision;
Many loved ones we will hurt to depart,
But we are not choosing our last mission;
Jesus decides, when our new life will start.

A new existance, eternal, so clearly defined,
To kneel in God's presence, such joy devine.

AGING

Enduring sounds of sweet life apart,
completes the silence of our being.
Creating memories to fill my heart,
looking forward to dreams I'm seeing.

Wondering when a clear light will shine,
visions of bright angels soaring above.
Placing thoughts in a very old mind,
whispers of messages, about God's love.

Changes of values, revered by many,
struggling and searching, souls far away.
Meaningful signs, of infinite plenty,
lonely thoughts prevail, as I cannot stay.

My mind linked to moments of a full life,
winding roads complete the extended stay.
Soothing new sounds, of the musicians fife,
on knotty knees I'm beginning to pray.

Great remorse, finds no visual support,
with expressions of fear, seeing the end.
Life was too short I eagerly report,
repeating best wishes, for all my friends.

Searching in places not really known;
longing to see the meaning of it all.
My savior must hear my soulful moan,
ending in heaven, our precious God calls

God's loving arms, my prayer for exposure.
finds ending for long awaited closure.

HOLY AND PURE

We must be Holy and Pure, to go there,
His perfect domain, a glorious place.
No sadness, anger, only One who cares,
spiritual splendor, when we see His face.

In today's world, can one be successful,
In following our Lord's, perfect commands?
Events can often, become so stressful,
it's hard to follow, His simple demands.

Life can be simple, when filled with God's grace,
no reason to fear, not reaching his Throne.
Know with His help, we shall soon see His face,
living for Him, we will not be alone.

The written Word, gives unfailing advice,
Holy and Pure, our God's plan does suffice.

FINISHING

My last poem, will be presented today,
as I have no more earthly things to do.
Enjoying a good life, it's time to say,
a greater calling, I now must pursue.

To see sweet Jesus, and so many friends,
approaching God, with great expectations.
I'm sure the Lord, has forgiven my sins,
His judgments are not, for my speculation.

My Savior has spoken, my time is here,
to meet in His home, so often described,
as a heavenly place, that will be so dear.
My joy is complete, my time has arrived.

I no longer live, in chaos on earth.
Eternal blessings, I've gained with new birth.

Printed in the United States
By Bookmasters